UNIVERSAL
TRUTHS

ESSAYS ON LIFE, FAMILY, AND BUSINESS

BY JAN SEMBA

Prominence Publishing

www.prominencepublishing.com

The author can be reached as follows: www.jansemba.com

Universal Truths/Jan Semba -- 1st ed.

ISBN: 978-1-988925-86-8

For my children – Jesse, Josh, and Max

ACKNOWLEDGEMENTS

In gratitude, I thank the following people:

My parents, without whom this book would never have happened.

My grandfather and grandmother, who taught me whatever you do, do with love.

My sister, who coached my nephews to exercise restraint and empathy with their zany uncle.

My clients, who trust me to work with them through thorny challenges which ultimately formed the grist for many of the essays.

Suzanne and Beth, who guided me through the design, formatting, and publishing process in record time and with great consideration and efficiency.

My dear friends, E and L, for fellowship over the years in matters of family, love, the insanity in life, and re-establishing equilibrium during the drama de jour.

Elisabeth, who has been my partner and companion from the beginning of the Covid pandemic and whose encouragement to make lemonade from lemons nudged me over the line to complete this book.

And, to Charlie. The living reminder that a dog is man's best friend and who has helped me to re-discover true unconditional love while ruminating over these universal truths.

WHAT PEOPLE ARE SAYING ABOUT THE AUTHOR

"My brother and I couldn't see eye to eye, and it seemed we couldn't agree on anything. Our father was CEO and "king," and felt the conflict. We were frustrated and not sure if we could continue to work together.

I reached out to several professional advisors, but none of them understood the real cause of my frustration.

From my first conversation with Jan, I knew – 'That's the guy'. From the start, he identified the challenges in our family dynamic and immediately focused on our communication and decision making.

He completely gets the integration of business and family. Seven years later, our family business has reached new levels of success and he continues to be instrumental in keeping our business family together."

Gino Melatti, Managing Partner
Groupe Melatti and Epik Hotels
Montreal

"When we retained Jan, my biggest objective was alignment. We have good, smart people, and Jan helped us harness the young ambition of the third generation with the great experience of the second generation for us to go down uncharted territory while keeping our culture intact."

"I learned from Jan how to facilitate a group of family and non-family members and to ensure the stakeholders' voices are heard. Becoming the glue, taking into account the thoughts of my father, my uncles, and the other team members allowed me to successfully step into the leadership role. Jan listens to and advocates for the younger generation."

"With his help, we created structures for decision making and governance that have supported the business as it has grown and evolved."

Anthony Broccolini, Chief Operating Officer
Broccolini
Montreal, Ottawa, Toronto

"I've known and worked with Jan for over ten years and have used his expertise in two places of employment for multiple projects. Jan is a strategic thinker, is thorough in approach, and due to his organizational intervention we have resolved a number of internal issues and charted positive proactive planning strategies that encompass hundreds of employees."

Janet Waldron, Chief Financial Officer
University of Maine and former Commissioner of
Administration and Finance for then Governor, now
United States Senator Angus King

CONTENTS

INTRODUCTION

People are all part of the whole – part of the cosmos, part of the universe, part of this world, part of the species of homo sapiens.

This book is for any and all people. The patterns and themes between these covers are universal. They are common to the human experience.

As a son, brother, partner, and father; as teammate; manager; business owner; family business partner; and family business advisor, my reflections over 50 years of experiences have been grouped here according to 16 patterns and themes.

My hope is for the reader to find resonance and common ground in the very moment – in this very moment.

Just as the oak tree in its strength and majesty is already present in the acorn, so too each of us possess the resources within us to successfully navigate the mysteries of life.

These reflections were recorded at different times over the past 20 years and represent universal truths as I discovered and stumbled on to them.

Offered with compassion and humility as we each live the human condition together, in our own and unique way.

WHATEVER YOU DO, DO WITH LOVE

As the last year passes behind us and a new year stands before us, have we taken the opportunity to reflect upon what went well for us in the past 12 months and what might have gone better?

Have we considered just what it is that we want more of—personally and professionally—and what it is that we want less of?

And, as we look ahead to the next 12 months, do we have a crystal-clear view of what we want and of what we don't want?

The process isn't always intuitive. Often, we sense that simply knowing what we want will suffice. We sense that we'll create the path as we move in the general direction of our desired outcome.

And, how often do we take the time to sit and reflect upon the outcomes that we would value most when the year ahead comes to an end?

Twelve months ago, my reflection took me to a vision of my 10-year-old daughter spending a weekend interacting and swimming with dolphins in a warm saltwater lagoon in the sunshine.

Today, I have the memory of an unforgettable smile as she surfed across the water, holding a dorsal fin in her hand while a dolphin gave her a ride. And the smile in the photograph in front of me is the same smile that I hold in my mind's eye.

It's the prior year's outcome I value most. And it would never have happened if I hadn't engaged in the process of looking ahead.

What would you like to experience in the next year? What would you like to achieve? What would you like to attain and obtain? Who would you like to meet? Where would you like to go?

And what do you need to do to make it happen?

The process begins with us. Here and now. We get to choose. We get to make it happen.

Best wishes for a joyful and productive New Year!

VISION AND PURPOSE MATTER

Management guru Peter Drucker has said that there are only two questions for business people—"What business are you in?" and "How's business?"

I'll suggest that we add another question, and that's "How do you improve business, how do you improve your results?"

Drucker goes on to say that the only true purpose for a business is to produce and bring in customers. We accomplish this through marketing and innovation, by creating something of value and communicating that value to the customer.

Marketing and innovation are the business activities that produce revenue—all other activities are expenses.

Drucker is very clear on what the most important activities are for business people. Do you have the same clarity about why your organization is in business?

What do your key stakeholders want to attain or obtain? What do they seek to participate in and experience?

And, what role do you personally play in achieving those objectives?

W. Edwards Deming went to Japan with General Douglas MacArthur after the end of World War II and was instrumental in rebuilding Japan. Companies around the world have successfully used Deming's management philosophies on quality and process improvement for many decades.

One of Deming's theories is the theory of optimization.

He states that: "You should never do anything unless you get the maximum yield, the maximum benefit for the minimum waste and the minimum effort."

If you're going to do anything, why do it for the minimum outcome when you can do it for the maximum outcome? A lack of clarity about where you're heading, where the organization is headed, and what you specifically hope to attain will absolutely preclude achieving maximum outcome with the least waste and effort.

Creating and defining a clear vision and mission and communicating a clear purpose throughout the organization is the fundamental cornerstone for operational productivity. Taking the time to define and plan will offset the reactive crisis management that follows from tactical initiatives that are not linked to an operationalized strategic plan.

Determining what the business needs to do to get the stakeholders to where they want to be and creating clearly defined critical factors for success that are tied to concrete action steps—these continue the process towards organizational success.

Does the business need more customers, or does it need more profitable business from existing customers? Does it need to develop a different type of customer than its traditional customer?

Should the business expand into new lines of business and take advantage of new opportunities for growth? Or should it focus on existing core competencies and even narrow its focus?

Does the business need more revenue, or can it grow its profitability by expanding profit margins through increased productivity?

We all suffer from spending valuable time on unimportant activities. Distinguishing the important from the insignificant is a fundamental by-product of the strategic planning process.

What are the few things that will make the most significant difference in your organization's success?

What are the few things that will make the most significant difference for your personal success?

Investing the time to reflect now will reward you in the future.

Recommended Reading: Deming, W. Edwards (2012) *The Essential Deming*. McGraw Hill. Drucker, Peter (1954) *The Practice of Management*. Harper & Brothers.

DON'T MISTAKE THE MAP FOR THE TERRITORY

Most of us are natural goal setters.

We make to-do lists, and we make plans for the upcoming weekend or our summer vacation.

Many businesses and organizations start with an idea that evolves into a plan.

A budget may support the plan.

As the organization grows and develops, plans are created to outline strategy and tactical operations, and charts create images of structure, workflow, and processes.

When an outsider asks to see how things look, a profit and loss statement, a balance sheet, a strategic plan, and an organizational chart illustrate the entity graphically—in much the same way as a map will define and describe geography.

Setting off on a journey, we refer to a map or program our GPS to show the way.

Embarking on a hike, we'll examine a map and look for signs and reference points to help us find our way.

These guides and illustrations are helpful tools to gain an understanding and perspective of the territory we are heading into.

And, they may not tell the actual story.

The map is distinct from the territory. It may or may not show if the route is under repair or if a detour is in place due to an accident or construction.

It won't inform us of the erratic driver in front of us, the convoy of school buses en route to the tournament, or the line of motor homes heading on vacation.

Yesterday, I hiked a mountain.

Though the map marked the route, it didn't point out how muddy the trail would be from the rain that had fallen the previous night.

The map didn't show how constantly the westerly wind was blowing nor the periodic gusts that would knock me off balance.

Nothing on the map indicated the family of grouse that would cross the trail in front of me, nor the deer that cautiously watched me through a grove of trees as I made my way upwards.

And the map did not warn me of the storm clouds that suddenly blew in from the west, causing me to race down the mountain to almost beat the downpour that drenched me even as the shelter of my car came into sight.

Just as maps show us a path forward from where we are to our intended destination, project plans, annual plans, and strategic plans identify the factors required to achieve our desired outcomes successfully.

And, we can anticipate that the environment around us will provide unexpected conditions that will require us to reconsider and adjust.

EXPECT THE UNEXPECTED

Several days ago, I was making a list and looking ahead to the upcoming weekend. My eldest son's birthday was approaching, and my thoughts and energy were focused on preparing a little celebration in the hope of providing him with some joy and happiness.

Being an active adolescent, he was clear on his menu preferences—seafood and steak. When asked what kind of cake he wanted, he was equally clear—dark chocolate with dark chocolate icing. During that conversation, he mentioned in passing that he wanted to ask a friend along for the weekend. I made a mental note to buy an additional pound of shrimp and steak.

I awoke on Friday morning with a cough and a bit of aching in my muscles, decided to pass on my morning workout, and took a handful of echinacea. By the time I picked the kids up from school, the cough was louder, deeper, and accompanied by sneezing, and the muscle aches made themselves known despite the ibuprofen I'd taken.

Driving into the mountains as darkness fell and the snow began to shine in the headlights, I started to make peace with the inevitable—I was getting sick for the first time this winter. And with a carload of kids and a birthday celebration planned. And, as the lone adult—chef and chauffeur—I was seriously sucking wind.

Whether in our personal or professional lives, we can have a high degree of confidence that our plans will encounter a circumstance outside our control. Something unpredictable or unexpected that will make us uncomfortable and challenge the roadmap we've drawn for ourselves.

Coming down with the flu just as you begin two days of skiing with four kids and the breakfasts and packing lunches, orchestrating dinners and washing dishes and negotiating bedtimes—trying to maintain equilibrium and good humor and forbearance through the headache and body shakes—it wasn't in the plan. But here we are. Uncomfortable, humbled, and more than just a little done in.

We might wish that things were different. Ask that health and strength be restored. But here we are. Worn out and undone.

Consider the key team member who resigns just as we're in the middle of a "can't fail" project with all the rest of the team already carrying their weight and then some.

Or the project that has been carefully planned and modeled financially to be on budget and on schedule just as long as it's completed in 24 months. And today, you learn that it won't be brought in until 30 months from now. The extra six months carrying costs are for your department to bear, by the way.

Where do we find the resources and resolve to overcome the unforeseen obstacles, those elements that we cannot control but that nevertheless show up and stand between us and our objective?

We can rail against the winds of fate that blow illness or disruption or subversion, or natural disaster in our path. It can be a tsunami, influenza, a conniving colleague, or falling off your bike.

We can grow upset, frustrated, angry. And yet, here we are.

On a continuum, most of us aren't asked to recover from a tsunami in our lifetime. But, many of us will get ill on the day of an important event.

Accepting each moment for what it is, acknowledging that it may not be what we want for ourselves, recognizing that things don't look the way we hoped they'd look, and still being able to lean into the discomfort and not turn and run from it, having the certainty that we have all the resources within us to overcome and thrive, there lies our solace.

Being clear on where we want to go, having a well-constructed roadmap highlighting possible obstacles and outlining solutions to overcome them, realistically assessing our resources and capital, that gets us part of the way there.

Remembering to authentically access our reservoirs of resilience, perseverance, patience, and flexibility in the face of large immovable objects and unpleasant conditions will shed light on a path both around and through.

The kids tell me the skiing was great and the cake was
pretty good, too.

WE CAN ONLY CONTROL OUR SIDE OF THE EQUATION

Control is our intention to establish predictability in our lives.

We build roofs to keep the rain from drenching us, walls to keep the wind from blowing us, fires to keep us warm, and make the dark light.

Our automobiles and airplanes have steering wheels, brakes, and throttles.

Stoves and ovens, phones and computers all have controls to turn on, turn off, and adjust.

Things are easier to control than elements, and people are difficult to control though we continue to try.

Families have rules; organizations have policies, processes, and procedures; societies have laws.

Humans try to control their environment to nurture and preserve the desirable and reduce and eliminate the undesirable.

Control can be understood as a power in the face of the elements—power to have more of what we want and less of what we don't want.

For some, this desire is extremely powerful and can impose its will in a variety of forms.

For a while.

There are aspects of life we can influence and even control.

And there are aspects of life that we can't control even with all our will, desire, ingenuity, power, and wealth.

Consider this.

We sit in a sailboat along an ocean's coast.

Our environment consists of the sky, the horizon, the ocean around us, masses of land.

We can't dictate or control day or night; clouds or blue sky; rain, snow, sleet; the strength of the wind or its direction; the ebb and flow of the tide; the size or frequency of the waves; the direction or strength of the current.

On the other hand, we can control how we want to set our sail, how we choose to hold the tiller and point the rudder, choose the point on the horizon we want to arrive at.

We journey on, adjusting our sail and rudder as the elements dictate, continuing on our course to a destination of our choosing.

We control what we can, beginning with a decision to start by managing ourselves, acknowledging that though we can't control the elements, we can control how we respond to them.

And, we can only control and manage our side of the equation.

The other person is going to do what they will.

How we act and react is up to us.

WE CAN CREATE SOMETHING FROM NOTHING

Innovation and creativity emerge as we enter into the unfamiliar and the unknown.

The familiar and known support and sustain, comfort and provide safety and predictability.

Our home offers a reliable refuge in which to rest and regroup.

We venture forth either along well-trodden paths and habituated patterns or with a roadmap highlighting direction, destinations, and options.

Exploring territory that is unfamiliar and unknown yields unpredictable experiences requiring greater attention to the present moment.

We cannot rely on our auto-pilot and habits to guide us through.

Dangers are enhanced.

Our reflexes and intuition will take precedence over memory and habit.

We enter the new and different and need to be awake to new possibilities.

When the old ways no longer suffice, when they fall short of producing the desired result or outcome, we will be required to dig deeper to shift our focus, to change our approach and orientation.

Pushing harder at the same, returning to the old, will only yield more of what we've been producing.

Letting our mind and body explore the unfamiliar, un-comfortable though it may seem and feel, reinventing, creating anew, there lies the opportunity for positive change.

Do we turn inward or outward to innovate?

Where does inspiration originate?

Who monitors the source—memory or imagination?

What creates the imagining?

Something new can only arise as we turn from the known.

Nothing new is in the known.

There is no unknown in the known.

Innovation occurs in moving from the known and com-fortable and habituated into the unknown, uncomfort-able, and unexperienced.

Innovation requires embracing change.

A dynamic move away from the current state.

And, it's so gratifying to create something from nothing.

UNDERSTANDING IS NOT THE SAME AS KNOWING

We think and believe the lesson is learned.

Then we blunder and the same lesson continues.

These lessons are universal.

Managing/controlling anger.

Self-absorption.

Disregarding the needs of others.

Succumbing to self-destructive tendencies.

Drifting from what we hold true.

Forsaking our boundaries and limits.

Giving our power over to others.

Hubris in believing we have it mastered.

Losing sight of what really matters.

Allowing ourselves to be overwhelmed.

Losing the present moment for the tyranny of hindsight or the desire to control outcomes.

Allowing fear to govern.

Being influenced by the masses.

Each of us has a central lesson to master in this lifetime.

A theme or a pattern that recurs, catching us unaware.

We return to meet it and live it.

It exhausts us.

It frustrates us.

It haunts us, returning when we least expect it or when we are most vulnerable.

It is our lesson to learn.

Until we get it right.

LIFE IS A MYSTERY

Many of us think of a mystery as a puzzle to be solved, a whodunit.

Our relationship with others, the everyday and extraordinary events that touch us or consume us, the challenges and opportunities that confront us.

We wonder, what can we do to achieve the desired state, the desired outcome, the best solution?

How do we solve this mystery of achieving more wealth, better health, the solution to our most pressing predicament?

What must I do to solve this and make it right?

This life of ours isn't a mystery to be solved.

We can't anticipate the next earthquake, the next tsunami, the next pandemic.

We can't determine when interest rates will go up or when our child or parent will get ill and need us to stay home to nurture them to good health.

It isn't incumbent upon us to solve the mystery of our life but rather to understand and accept that each life is a mystery. We as characters and participants need only do our very best in the present moment as the events and circumstances around us continue to unfold.

LOSS IS NORMAL

Every four years, much of the world shifts its focus for four weeks in June and July and turns its attention to teams from 32 countries as they put forth their best efforts to win soccer's World Cup. The very finest practitioners of a profession emerge on stage to orchestrate and collaborate for all the world to see. Unashamed, in a naked desire to demonstrate mastery of their craft with the ambition of claiming victory for their side, their country, and for themselves.

Of the 23 players on each of the teams—736 master craftsmen in all—only 23 will emerge with the ultimate prize.

All 736 can claim a life of work—of sweat, pain, toil, and sacrifice—in honing their skill, striving to develop their natural gifts to the fullest, overcoming challengers, enduring and persevering. But of those 736, a mere three percent will be acknowledged as members of the team that lifts the World Cup.

What of the other 97 percent? They have prepared, competed, and fallen short.

Or have they?

To a certain extent, soccer's World Cup is a zero-sum game. Thirty-two challengers, but only one champion.

Viewed in this way, the vast majority of the participants will be viewed as having been ultimately unsuccessful. Here in the United States, our representatives were unable to prevail in a single match during the tournament, fortunate to have scored a single goal on their own. Finishing last in their group and 26th of the 32 participants. Successful or unsuccessful?

Consider the everyday expectations concerning success and failure that we encounter in the workplace, at home, and in society in general.

We either land the new customer or lose them to the competition. We get the new promotion or lose out to one of our colleagues. The request for a loan to fund our business expansion is approved by the bank or turned down. Our children make the honor roll or fail to get the grades necessary for the award. The offer we make for our dream house is either accepted or rejected by the seller.

Our boss sarcastically dismisses our suggestion during a staff meeting. A colleague smirks and shakes her head in agreement. We commit a faux pas at a cocktail party and catch our neighbors laughing about it at the grocery store. At a parent-teacher conference, we're told that our child is unable to keep up with the class and that an evaluation for a learning disability is recommended.

Society tells us to be proud of our successes and accomplishments. Magazine covers tout the 500 wealthiest among us, the 100 largest companies, the "man of the year."

But how are we to act when we fall short, when we don't prevail, when we're reminded that our behavior is not in keeping with the social norm?

Consider the three Swiss soccer players who yesterday had a chance to be successful. After 90 minutes, their game with Ukraine was still tied 0-0. Fatigued, the teams continued in the 90-degree heat through a 30-minute overtime. Still tied 0-0 after two hours of running.

The match was to be decided by penalty kicks, essentially the equivalent of shooting free throws in basketball.

With 45,000 in the stadium, with their countrymen and tens of millions watching television throughout the world, five players from each team prepared to step to the penalty spot, face the goalkeeper, and shoot the most automatic shot in soccer.

Inexplicably, the first three Swiss players all missed their chances, while three of the four Ukrainians made theirs and won the match. And, the Ukrainian who missed his chance was signed by an English club for a $56 million transfer fee and had been named European Footballer of the Year.

The Ukrainians could celebrate their achievement with pride—their first trip to the World Cup and advancing to the quarterfinals.

But what of those three Swiss, each one a master craftsman? Representing their countrymen on their profession's largest stage and falling short. Disappointment? Embarrassment? Humiliation?

As each of us walks our personal path striving to be the best we can be, inevitably we slip and fall, we jump to reach the other side only to come up short and end up wet and muddy, or we inadvertently fall into some muck that may or may not be of our own making.

We all stumble. We all fall. Sometimes for all the world to see. More often, we sheepishly look around to reassure ourselves that no one has witnessed our vulnerability while we cling to our cloak of pride.

Where others may see humiliation, perhaps we can find humility. Humility in the knowledge that ours is the human condition. And feel compassion for our humanity. For success is not a zero-sum game. And even master craftsmen—the very best of the best—come up short from time to time.

COMMUNICATION MATTERS MOST

Dialogue, Discussion, and Debate

"What we have here is a failure to communicate."
—Paul Newman in Cool Hand Luke

The fundamental building block of any interpersonal system—whether family, business enterprise or institution—is the relationship between individuals. How well we understand each other directly affects our ability to coexist harmoniously, productively, and cooperatively.

Our ability to listen, empathize and comprehend forms one side of the communication equation. Clearly expressing our ideas, feelings, and observations in a respectful and considerate manner forms the other side of the equation.

These are elementary concepts, well known and understood by all of us. So why do we encounter conflict and miscommunication in our relationships? And why are families and organizations rampant with people profoundly upset with each other?

Most of our verbal and written communication takes the form of conversation—whether in person or by telephone, by letter, memo, text, e-mail, or PowerPoint presentation. In conversation, we make our ideas and feelings known and we express our needs, hopes, and demands.

Our conversation generally appears as discussion, debate, or dialogue. The mode we use in any given interaction largely determines the way in which our message is received, and it influences the quality of the relationship that we're engaged in.

Discussion has the same root as "percussion" and "concussion." It means "to break things up," emphasizing the notion of analysis, where many different points of view exist, and everyone is presenting a different one. It's like a tennis game in which ideas are batted back and forth and the intent is to win or to get points for yourself. In discussion, I tell you what I think and you tell me what you think.

Debate takes on a different flavor. Its derivation translates as "to beat" or "to batter." It implies a contest, strife, an argument. In debate, we defend and attack. Its desired outcome is zero-sum—I win, and you lose. It does not contemplate a win-win solution.

The physicist, David Bohm, explains that "dialogue" comes from the Greek "dialogos." "Logos," meaning "the word" or "the meaning of the word," and "dia" meaning "through." Bohm suggests that this evokes the image of a stream of meaning flowing among and through and between us. Holding on to this image opens the possibility that some new understanding may emerge between the participants.

In dialogue, nobody is trying to win. Rather, we bring to the relationship the possibility that something new and more dynamic may emerge as a result of our engagement with one another. Everybody wins if anybody wins. And, if a mistake is discovered on the part of anybody, everybody gains. Here we are not playing against each other but with each other. Win-win is possible.

As we consider our day-to-day encounters with the members of our family, with our friends, with our colleagues and counterparts, with our customers and clients, what form of communication do we predominately engage in? How conscious are we of the way in which we craft our message or respond to others?

And are we consciously or unconsciously driving our personal agenda forward at the expense of a more dynamic possibility that might emerge from greater collaboration with others?

Discussion, debate, and dialogue. How we elect to engage impacts our personal and professional success, the success of those we lead and manage, the success of our family, our business, and the organization we represent. Our choices determine what we are known as, how we are thought of, and the welcome we receive from those with whom we interact.

Conflict or harmony, combat or collaboration, success or frustration. The choice is largely ours. More of the same, or something better? It's up to you.

Recommended Reading: Bohm, David (1996). *On Dialogue*. Routledge/Taylor and Francis.

PREPARE, PERFORM, REFLECT

At a competitive level, a three-part process of preparation, performance, and reflection characterizes all sports. This process is common to individual sports such as skiing, golf, tennis, or running marathons and to team sports such as soccer, baseball, volleyball, or hockey. Concert musicians also experience a similar process.

During the preparation phase, skills, strength, stamina, strategy, and tactics are developed. Practice and training regimens occur daily or several times daily and the period of preparation lasts weeks or months.

The actual performance or competition is brief in comparison to the time and energy spent in preparing. Matches, meets, races, or games range from a few seconds to 60 or 90 minutes or several hours, and in the case of tournaments and Olympic Games, continue over several days.

Whether performed before an international audience, for a grandstand of spectators or just in the presence of judges and competitors, the performance is the anticipated culmination of the training and practice and preparation phase.

Following the performed event, athletes review and reflect upon their performance. Videotapes and recordings can offer a frame-by-frame analysis of each aspect of the contest. Debriefings with coaches and teammates as well as individual reflection provide a basis for integrating "lessons learned" in an effort to improve future performance.

As we turn an eye to our professional endeavors and how we manage our business or career, we generally encounter very different ratios of preparation and reflection to performance. Other than the quarterly directors' meeting, a potentially high yield sales call, a presentation to analysts or a trade group, or a meeting with the boss to discuss a raise, preparation generally gives way to everyday performance.

And who has time for reflection except when we look to see whether or not we've hit this month's numbers or whether we're on budget? When is the last time we ran a "frame by frame" replay of our daily performance and listed our "lessons learned"?

In the organizational context, preparation is often analogous with training, and, once we're deemed proficient, our ongoing training is often relegated to maintaining our licensing or professional credentials. While in the athletic arena, we spend more time preparing than performing, our daily work lives are almost exclusively characterized by performance.

With the year winding down and a new calendar on the horizon, we're served up a natural opportunity to reflect upon our performance and our successes and also to note and reflect upon those areas in which we've fallen short this year.

And, here stands an opportunity to open our minds to that which we might create and live into over the next 12 months.

What are the two or three most important things you'd like to achieve professionally? What can you do personally to most move your organization forward? What would you like to experience in your personal life and what stands in the way of where you are and where you'd like to be next December?

Reflection gives us the opportunity to prepare with purpose toward clear and meaningful goals and to ensure that our performance is truly moving us most efficiently and productively in the direction we want to go.

RESISTANCE IS NORMAL

We encounter resistance in virtually all aspects of life. It crops up externally—in the people and things around us—as well as internally, in ourselves.

Resistance is the cause of endless frustration and conflict. It drains energy and reduces productivity and joy. Resistance is ubiquitous and yet so few individuals and organizations understand it, and fewer still deal with it effectively.

Why?

Resistance appears when we want one thing and someone wants another. We want our child to eat spinach or green beans. Our child resists. We want our spouse or partner to help with a project or take a trip to a particular place. They resist. We want the customer to buy our product. They resist. The organization wants to deliver its service in a new way. Employees within the organization and customers and vendors outside the organization resist.

We want one thing. They want another. We want them to see it our way. They don't want to see it our way.

We want them to change. They want us to go away. We push for change. They resist.

What causes this dynamic?

The catalyst for resistance is change. Change implies that we act differently from how we have been acting.

Unless and until we can see, feel, understand, and know why it's in our best interest to embrace the change, we will be inclined to resist. In other words, we first need to be sufficiently motivated to change.

But motivation on its own is usually insufficient to dissolve resistance. Why?

Human beings are creatures of habit. We rely on certain routines in our daily lives to improve our productivity and routine allows us to make a series of tasks almost automatic.

When you regularly do your daily sit-ups at the same time every morning, you don't have to think about them. It becomes as habitual as brushing your teeth or taking a shower.

Most of us are comfortable in our habits, and, as we all know, habits are hard to break.

It's natural for us to resist events that may disrupt our lives—even if the change is for positive reasons yielding positive results.

So, motivation isn't enough to dissolve resistance. We also need to acquire the skills to change—the skills to change our habits, our attitude, our beliefs, our behavior.

What are these skills?

Because of our inclination toward habituation, we need to become skilled not only in stopping the old habit. We also need to develop the skill of replacing the old habit with a new behavior. Eliminating the old is insufficient. Without a new behavior to replace it, we will revert to the old way, particularly at times of stress or inattentiveness.

This skill of replacing the old with the new applies not only to physical behavior, but to mental behavior as well. Our attitudes are habits of thought, and they respond similarly to our physical habits and routines.

Understanding and appreciating the dynamics of our human tendency regarding "change" can transform our daily lives—both personally and professionally.

On the personal side, consider the habit of staying up too late and waking up tired in the morning. Or eating pastries instead of fruit. Or surfing the Internet instead of going for a walk or run. Or tuning out instead of truly engaging with our kids or partner.

In the business context, significant energy and resources are expended in planning, analyzing, developing, constructing, and implementing a new organizational alignment, a new system, process, procedure, production facility, business expansion or contraction.

Yet how many of us have been part of projects that have left us frustrated and exasperated because of discord, conflict, and disappointing end results?

Almost every project we implement in the business world will cause someone's workflow to change. Unless and until that person is aware that she will need to change, unless and until he is motivated to change, unless and until they integrate a new behavior to replace the old behavior, we will experience sub-optimal results.

We can experience resistance in the form of conflict, discord, disagreement, and lack of alignment.

Whether it's a software conversion, a relocated or expanded facility, a cultural change initiative, or something as seemingly simple as a new policy or procedure, the human tendency to resist change will rear its head.

Will we need to drive the change down into the organization? Or will we have taken the time to invite an awareness of the need to change, given others the opportunity to motivate themselves and embrace the change, and provided them with the necessary skills to modify their behavior and align to the change (training/ development)?

Understand resistance.

Because, in this world, change is the only constant.

And, resistance is normal.

WE HAVE WHAT IT TAKES TO BE HAPPY

Every person possesses the resources to successfully navigate any circumstance life presents.

Just as the oak tree is already in the acorn, the whole has enfolded within it the particular, and the particular has enfolded within it the whole.

Begin to consider that we each have the resources of the cosmos within us, just as the cosmos has us within it.

This genius within is there for us to access.

With resolve, consciousness, hope, and awareness, we open ourselves to the possibility that we can respond in this moment to that which demands a response.

We can respond in such a way that we can have success (as we describe success for ourselves) in this moment and this success will not be zero-sum, but rather it contains within it the potential for multiple win-win.

This genius response is at core expansive rather than restrictive.

It allows for multiple positive potentials, multiple positive outcomes.

It contains elements and aspects that can support and nurture a variety and myriad of possibilities rather than impose a limited range of acceptable or sub-optimal end results.

This genius response is inclusive rather than exclusive.

It stems from a collective I-Thou rather than I-It and a mutual respect and openness to dialogue.

These opportunities are found in virtually every encounter—as long as the encounter is relational and not transactional.

Recommended Reading: Buber, Martin (1970) *I and Thou*, Charles Scribner's Sons.

DRAMA DISTRACTS

What constitutes drama and where does it stem from? Why do we spend so much personal and organizational energy engaging in and unraveling the unwanted dramas that others bring to our lives?

And, why, as leaders, do we acknowledge, condone, enable, and perpetuate drama in the relationships for which we are responsible?

Drama is defined as an exciting series of events, an episode that is turbulent or highly emotional, a situation in real life having the progression or emotional effect characteristic of a play.

How can we recognize drama, and how can we begin to manage it out of our lives and out of our workplace?

Drama appears as a "story," as a historical occurrence which the storyteller feels compelled to bring into the present. By acknowledging the story, we enable the perpetuation of the historical into the present and in doing so, we support the energy (usually negative) of what has occurred and passed before.

And, to what end?

How are we, or they, helped in any way by revisiting the emotional content of what has come before?

Acknowledging current pain or suffering by engaging in compassion, empathy, tolerance, love, respect, or generosity seems appropriate. Extending our appreciation of the human condition when confronted with loss and the associated pain of death, divorce, unemployment, or other undesirable life events serves to affirm our common humanity.

And some life events take on Shakespearean or even Biblical qualities—consider those wrongfully incarcerated or islanders stranded after a tsunami.

But in our daily lives, such dramas are thankfully few.

More common are the "did you hear the client cancelled the London project and it sounds like Michael is going to get canned for it..." or "can you believe Jessica's ex is filing for custody of the kids?" or" how could they possibly promote Andrew over Sarah or Megan?"

How often do we hear about these dramas in the workplace, from our colleagues, employees, and customers, and how often do we get drawn into them?

And how much time do we, as managers, spend listening to our direct reports share their dramas and woes, their trials and tribulations, their accusations and defenses, and what approach do we use to resolve the discord?

The other day I sat in the stands watching my 16-year-old son play in a high school soccer match. The game was quite one-sided, and with a couple of minutes left to go, as my son played the ball to a teammate, a player from the losing side ran through him. Looking up from the ground, my son sought out the referee for acknowledgment of the foul, but the referee had followed the ball and missed the collision completely.

Words were spoken between the players as they ran beside each other, trailing the play. I watched my son shoulder check his opponent and more words were exchanged. The final whistle soon sounded and the players left the field.

After the coach's post-game talk, the players walked toward the parking lot. Still emotionally charged, my son's first words to me were, "Boy, that kid was lucky the whistle blew. I was going to nail him".

Needless to say, the conversation during our car ride home revolved around restraint, anger management, the role frustration and humiliation play in generating aggression and conflict, and the downside risk of running up a score and humiliating another party.

These concepts are not always self-evident, and "being right" seems to justify our emotional edge and indignation. Dramatic incidents punctuate our lives as leaders, managers, colleagues, partners, parents, and neighbors.

And, though dramatic moments occur from time to time, ongoing dramas steal focus and energy and inhibit performance.

How?

Most fundamentally, dramas shift our focus away from the activities that move us most powerfully from where we are to where we want to be. Dramas distract us from the task at hand.

But, as leaders and managers, dramas can often become the task at hand. Intervening with an upset employee, an irate or dissatisfied customer, or a member of the media digging for a juicy story can suddenly become the issue of the moment. Managing ourselves and our team through these dramas becomes central just so that we can return to keeping our lives and our business operations on course.

So, we take the time and do it.

But how much time and energy could be more productively used if workplace drama was minimized or eliminated?

"Impossible!" you say.

And, perhaps not.

If our workplace were to become a "drama-free zone," how much more productive, positive, and on purpose might we and our teams and colleagues become?

How often do we think—"there just aren't enough hours in a day"? And how many hours do we spend engaging in or managing drama?

Take a hard look at the drama factor that touches your life. Opportunity might lie just ahead...

GENIUS LIES WITHIN

We don't create genius by bolstering our weaknesses.

We create genius by playing to our strengths.

Each of us possesses natural abilities.

Some abilities are stronger than others.

As an example, there are multiple abilities in how we take in information—in how we learn.

Some of us learn best by listening.

Others learn best by reading.

Some of us learn best by examining a drawing, a chart, or a graph.

And some of us learn best kinesthetically—through movement, rhythm, and physically engaging with the information.

A way to consider this is how a coach informs an athlete or a group or team of athletes.

She might say, "we will move from left to right and Player 1 is responsible for moving first".

And she might write, "we will move from left to right and Player 1 is responsible for moving first".

And, she might go to the blackboard or whiteboard and draw the position of the players, indicating they would move from left to right and highlighting that Player 1 would move first.

And, she might take the group to the field, assemble them in the proper position or formation, and then have the movement from left to right occur, repeating and correcting as necessary.

Each of us learns using these natural processes.

And, generally, we each have an ability to learn that is stronger and more natural than the other ways of learning.

It doesn't mean we can't learn through the other channels, rather that it's easier to learn using our preferred natural learning channel.

Identifying our strongest natural abilities is the path for releasing the genius within.

GOOD HEALTH IS GOOD

What will most improve the health of the whole?

The parts that make up the whole are interconnected.

The sun rises and the rhythm of a new day begins.

We emerge from sleep into wakefulness, become aware of ourselves through our five senses and through the consciousness of being awake and alive.

We are each individual human beings, a complete working organism, and as we wake and rise, we stand on our feet—independent and whole.

Yet, we did not begin as independent individuals.

We were conceived from a union of two independent whole beings, each a complete whole, but incapable of reproducing on their own.

Our whole self was created by two whole selves—by two whole beings.

And, historically, our species has evolved and been nurtured through the family entity.

The family itself is comprised of a number of wholes—parents, children, siblings—which are further labeled grandparents, grandchildren, uncles, aunts, and cousins. Each entity is a whole while also part of a greater whole.

These are the building blocks and core elements of human society.

As we have evolved into tribes, communities, nations, and organizations, each begins with an individual whole and grows and expands to an entity—a whole onto itself.

This awareness allows us to consider a seminal universal question.

"What will most improve the health of the whole?"

Universal because it can apply to the individual whole.

Universal because it can apply to the societal or organizational whole.

Health is universal to all organisms.

In good health, we thrive, we grow, we bear fruit, we blossom, we multiply.

In poor health, we struggle, our well-being suffers, our existence is suboptimal, our attention and energy is drawn to healing or overcoming our affliction.

People have various forms of health.

In good physical health, we move effortlessly without discomfort.

We easily eat and digest the fuel our body requires.

Our sleep and rest refresh and rejuvenate our body and mind.

It is the rare person who never gets a fever, a rash, a strained muscle, or an upset stomach.

We consider these ailments "normal," an expected aspect of life.

Similarly, families, tribes, communities, nations, and organizations have various forms of health.

In good health, there is alignment between the various parts of the whole.

In poor health, there is conflict, disagreement, dispute, argument, fighting, and war.

In good health and in poor health, we can ask, examine, and reflect—"what will most improve the health of the whole?".

CHANGE IS
THE ONLY CONSTANT

We witnessed a dramatic shift in the United States the day Barack Obama was elected. An hour before midnight, scenes of jubilation and images of faces moved to tears of joy filled the airwaves. "I never thought I'd see this in my lifetime." "If only my parents could be here to see this." "So many died along the way in order for this day to come." Words from Americans with dreams of change finally seeing their dreams come true.

Truly historical turning points occur from time to time and touch us if we allow them to. In the past decades, we have experienced a handful of dramatic events that cause us to pause and reconsider the world as we've known it. The fall of the Berlin Wall. The end of apartheid. Terrorist attacks on September 11. Events that begin to change our landscape in profound and unexpected ways.

Historical events created by human beings that touch so many in deeply meaningful ways are rare. Yet each of our lives is marked by many important events that affect us in profound ways.

My seventeen-year-old son is preparing to graduate from high school this spring and to begin college in the fall. His graduation is an event that will represent accomplishment and completion to him, with the wildly anticipated freedom and independence of college life soon to come.

A child's graduation marks a relatively common event in the life of parents around the world. And our experience of this event is often quite different from our child's experience.

I, for one, already sense the loss of an active and constant presence in my household. Seventeen years of a lovable being interacting with me in an everyday and physically present way.

One of us anticipates the freedom and independence of the pending change; the other has a wistful longing to keep things as they have been.

(How often do we see and understand things one way only to be surprised or stunned that those around us have a completely different experience?)

And, change is the only constant.

This theme of change is universal, and the accompanying themes of resistance, opportunity and risk, desire for gain and fear of loss, excitement for the new and clinging to the known—these are universal as well.

Every organization and every family have its own historical turning points. The day a business is founded, the day a founder turns the reins over to the heir, the first acquisition, the great new product.

Businesses evolve from the entrepreneurial to the managerial, and some to the organizational. Family enterprise passes from generation to generation. The turning points only come to pass when the current state is replaced with a future state. For some, this happens in an intended manner. To the less fortunate, the turning points are unintended and unexpected.

With each acknowledgment that our current state of affairs can be improved and that a future state of affairs is more desirable, we embark on a quest for change. Implementing a new organizational structure, redefining or realigning a project team, hiring a new employee—each will trigger the themes of resistance, of desire and fear, of movement towards the new and clinging to and wishing for the old.

In some faces, we will see happiness, joy, relief, and celebration.

Others will be anxious, hesitant, and stressed.

These turning points can touch us deeply, and we are best served not to take them lightly

Our most important role is to acknowledge these changes and prepare ourselves and those around us to see and appreciate the opportunities for still greater success, for positive growth and the hope for a better and brighter future.

WE PREFER THE FAMILIAR TO THE UNFAMILIAR

The Road to Dodge

Every once in a while, we find ourselves in a circumstance that is uncomfortable, unpleasant, undesirable, and altogether familiar.

It's like waking up in the wild west town of Dodge and wondering how we got there.

For some, it begins with a difference of opinion with a friend, a loved one, or a co-worker.

The difference of opinion turns into a debate, heated discussion, argument, and takes on harsh tones or worse.

For others, it may be a casual drink that becomes two or more and morphs into a lost evening or weekend or bender.

The permutations and forms of unpleasant and undesirable are myriad, and yet the road to Dodge is universal.

Waking up as the hot sun burns our face and the thick coat of dust in our mouth reminds us of something ever so familiar.

We blink our eyes, and yes, sure enough, we see that we're in Dodge again.

And then, we begin to piece together some of the events and circumstances that once again led us to Dodge.

Many of us wake up in Dodge from time to time.

Occasionally, we catch a glimpse of a sign pointing down the road with bold letters –DODGE. Still, much as we don't like the place, we manage to wake up there.

Then, it can happen that seeing the sign reminds us that Dodge still lies ahead and it's not a place we like to end up in.

We begin to recognize the road, the tell-tale signs, the familiar habits and patterns that have conspired to take us to Dodge.

And we can choose to change if we want to.

Wake up in Dodge again?

GET COMFORTABLE WITH BEING UNCOMFORTABLE

Doing what we do, better. This lies at the core of performance improvement. Performance improvement implies creating and innovating a new and better way to be, act, or behave.

To do this, we need the freedom to experiment, try, and test. Some attempts to generate improvement will inevitably prove to be unsuccessful. So, we must have permission to fail in our attempts to be more successful. And we must have the courage to fall as we attempt to fly.

Yet, most societal, organizational and family cultures frown on mistakes. Supervisors often admit that they would prefer to perform a task themselves and know that it will be done right rather than delegate to a subordinate and risk the chance of a serious mistake.

This approach to risk avoidance is common in everyday life. When our children ask to bake cookies, we may decide to break the eggs into the bowl ourselves rather than risk the egg slipping from little fingers and exploding on the floor, creating a large-scale clean-up effort requiring adult intervention.

Or, we may choose to accompany the salesperson on the sales call because we know that we can close the deal but are unsure our salesperson can successfully do it on their own.

So, how does our desire to "do it right" or our drive to "avoid making a mess" affect creativity and innovation?

When we focus on "doing it right," we have an expectation of a desired result in mind. We may also have the expectation that the desired result will be achieved by following a specific process.

Baking cookies "the right way" may involve following the recipe and creating good tasting, eye-catching, aromatic cookies with a minimum of fuss and mess and with the kitchen already clean and orderly even while the cookies are cooling.

If the cookies have been eaten but the bowls and mixer are still covered in dough, and the counters and floor are white with flour, we may be more inclined to more closely supervise the process in the future and to more carefully decide which tasks to delegate and which to do ourselves.

By following the recipe and keeping to the process, we have a framework for achieving a predictable outcome. We can substitute raisins or butterscotch for chocolate chips and by keeping to the process, we can still ensure a predictable outcome.

But is it possible for us to bake an even more delicious and beautiful cookie? Can we do it by following the same recipe?

And can we improve the process so that we can bake our cookies faster, with less clean-up, and with fewer adults in the kitchen?

How will we know whether we can create a better cookie unless we try another recipe or come up with a new one of our own?

But this involves the risk that our next batch won't be as tasty or as pretty.

The more we desire a specific outcome, the more we want to control that outcome, and the more we need that outcome, the greater our tendency to grow risk averse.

If our boss is coming for dinner, and we plan on serving cookies for dessert, we are less likely to allow the kids to try a new cookie recipe and leave them alone in the kitchen to give it a go.

If we're entering the new fiscal year with a revenue forecast from corporate that we are confident we can meet, we may be less likely to try a new approach or replace an existing product or service with a new one and risk our year-end bonus.

If we're asked to submit an estimate to build a two-story, four-bedroom house similar to the one we completed last month, we'll typically create the estimate in much the same way we did for the last house.

Or will we?

If our estimate caused us to lose $50,000, perhaps we'll decide to make changes to our estimating process. Will we be more likely to change our approach if we lost money or if we made money?

Creativity and innovation are the inspiration and the process of making something new. They are the act of making different, making better, making changes.

Making changes for the better lies at the heart of performance improvement. Performance improvement is the art and practice of creating and innovating positive change.

In the realm of sport, we create positive change in the form of running or going faster; jumping farther or higher; lifting more; throwing farther, harder, or more accurately; hitting or kicking a ball more consistently to where we want it to go; or, eluding our pursuers more adroitly.

In business, we innovate positive change by providing our customers more of what they want faster, more efficiently, and for less cost and more profit; improving productivity; increasing results through others; heightening the satisfaction and delight our customers and employees experience and continuing to produce the greatest yield with the least amount of waste and the least amount of effort.

In our personal lives, we increase our happiness and satisfaction when we identify what makes us unhappy or dissatisfied and take the step of making a change for the better.

Creating and innovating positive change begins with deciding what we want more of and less of. We become more satisfied when we get off the couch, create more of what we want, and eliminate the stuff we recognize we don't want.

We can keep getting the results we've been getting by sticking to the old recipe and doing things the way we've always done them.

Or, we can be creative, take a chance, and innovate some positive change in our lives.

The art of performance improvement. It's often simple but rarely easy.

IF IT'S TRUE FOR ME, IT'S ALSO TRUE FOR YOU

There are many aspects common to us. Understanding common ground allows us to sit on the same side of the table rather than on opposite sides.

Universal elements transcend cultures, geographies, and historical times.

For all people, physical well-being is essential. We prefer to be healthy to being unhealthy.

For all people, fundamental economic/financial well-being is essential. We need food and shelter.

For virtually all adults, work and career are essential. We need to create, and we need to be active, mentally and physically.

Once we are born, our family helps us survive. This attachment continues in physical or psychological form throughout our lives

Humans are social creatures with various bonds that are affirmed and reaffirmed in contact with others, in family, in community.

Mental and spiritual well-being plays a central role in our ability to be peaceful and content and to enjoy happiness.

As we pass through the various stages of life—infancy, childhood, adolescence, adulthood, and the later years—these elements will at times hold more importance and at times less importance.

If we are healthy, we may focus more on improving our economic lot in life than on improving our health.

If we desire a partner and mate, the social aspect may seem more important.

Parents with infants may find the family aspect more compelling.

These elements are active either as conscious concerns or on a subconscious level in the form of desires or memories, needs and hopes, or aspects to avoid or minimize.

And these elements—physical, family, work/career, financial, social, community, mental, and spiritual —constitute the factors that determine our well-being.

We can examine how each element presents itself in our life at this moment, at this point in time. For each element, we can identify aspects we might want more of and aspects we might want less of.

We can reflect and explore the relative balance or imbalance we're experiencing in our lives, what changes would allow us to increase our happiness,

These universal characteristics help us reflect on what we're experiencing in life today and what we might prefer to experience in life in the days ahead, and how to allocate our time, energy, and resources to get more of what we want and less of what we don't want.

These insights can also be helpful in better understanding and communicating with others. We all share concerns about the various aspects that comprise our individual well-being.

Our ability to think, feel, and experience is universal.

Finding common elements to share our thoughts, feelings, and experiences softens barriers and hardened boundaries that define "us" and "them."

It is here that a previously unattainable "we" may be found.

Because, at a fundamental and universal level, if it's true for me, it's also true for you.

SURPRISES HAPPEN

A recent experience created an impact that will last a lifetime. Eastern wisdom reminds us that "when the student is ready, the teacher appears."

Several weeks ago, in a hotel room early on a bright Monday morning Victoria Day holiday in Canada, I experienced a sudden flash of white pain. My first thought was, "you've just had an aneurysm." My next thought was, "calm down; you're too dramatic; it's probably just a bad headache."

After a while of kneeling on the floor with my head on the bed, after tossing down a few Advil only to have them come flying back with equal speed, I decided to get some professional advice. On my first attempt, I managed to contact an internationally renowned medical practitioner, author, lecturer, friend, and client.

As I described the condition I found myself in, I was told, to my great relief, that more likely than not, I was experiencing a bad migraine, but that I should get my-self to a clinic and get checked out immediately.

In spite of, or precisely because of the pain in my head, my usually sound decision-making yielded to a rational-ization something along the lines of "you're in Canada, you have clients to see tomorrow, it's just a migraine, just sleep it off."

Which is what I tried to do.

By evening I had managed to pull out my laptop and e-mail all involved to cancel my next several days' com-mitments. It had become clear to me that I had one hell of a headache.

One day in the hotel became two, and by late morning Wednesday, I had enough. Rallying hard, I pulled my-self together, checked out, got in my car, and began the drive back home to Maine, where I intended to get in bed and not get up until my head stopped hurting.

Somewhere along the ride, a brilliant thought hit me. "Let me get a second opinion." Dialing up yet another friend, client, and in this case, an extremely accomplished sur-geon, I was met with the admonition that I get myself to a clinic. My friend, Chris, was so concerned that he told me he would meet me at my local hospital.

I drove on, crossed the border, cleared customs, and head-ed off to get my head examined. I frankly have little recall of that drive. Fortunately, it was a path well-trodden. My travels to meet prospective and current clients have taken me along that route several times a month for the past several years, and I was mainly operating on autopilot.

As I arrived at the hospital parking lot, some five hours after leaving the hotel, I called Chris to say that I felt something wasn't quite right because the 30 yards from my car to the emergency room had been quite an adventure. Chris was on the way, and I got to cool my heels in the waiting room for about half an hour even though, unlike emergency rooms in other parts of the world, this one was empty except for me.

Eventually, a physician's assistant evaluated me and was about to send me on my way when Chris arrived. I later learned that I had been diagnosed with the flu and would have been directed simply to drive the 45 minutes to my home to begin my convalescence.

Good fortune was on my side. Chris persuaded the emergency room staff that, despite their protestations, they put me through a CT scan.

As it has been described to me, it seems that the faces of the ER team turned a whiter shade of pale as they learned that my head was full of blood that wasn't supposed to be there.

I was politely informed that an ambulance would medevac me immediately to a hospital in Portland and that I ought not to be surprised that once there, I would further be transported to Boston because "they're not set up to handle what you've got."

Thankfully an IV was hooked up, the morphine began to flow, and the throbbing in my head receded from white pain to more manageable levels of ice picks twisting and turning through my skull. We began to move, and I began to ponder the essential question, "what is this lesson about?"

All this is the background to a simple yet profound thought and decision I made while in the ambulance.

I decided that no one would be invested in my health more than me. I also decided that all the medical staff I would come in contact with were truly there to help me regain my health. They would be committed and working to help me get better.

Essentially, I decided to rely on two fundamental human truths.

First, believe and trust in yourself. Second, believe and trust in the essential goodness of others, and believe that they will wish to help you succeed.

In addition to Chris's insistence that I get to the hospital, in addition to his help in getting the ER team to administer the scan against their better judgment, I have no doubt that the simple thoughts I came to in the ambulance saved my life and allowed me to recover far more rapidly than my neurosurgeon and the medical team initially thought possible.

The powerfully positive aspects of this experience allow me to spread this message in the years to come with the intention of helping others improve not only their ability to heal and maintain good health but also in continuing to achieve higher levels of success for themselves and those around them, personally and professionally.

If this can happen to me, it can happen to anyone.

What followed were three days in the intensive care unit, peaks and valleys of intense pain, intravenous cocktails of morphine and Dilaudid, hallucinations, and also caring and nursing of incredible warmth, concern, and consideration that I can attribute to the attitude I chose to adopt during my ambulance ride.

(My eighteen-year-old son has just finished telling me that his research shows that Dilaudid is eight times stronger per milligram than morphine and three times stronger than heroin. The things that interest kids these days!)

Early in the morning of my third day in intensive care, my neurosurgeon answered my question by telling me that I should expect to remain in the hospital recovering for another two to three weeks.

That thought itself was maddening and crazy making to me, and that day was probably the most trying and difficult.

I exhausted myself, undid much of the healing I had achieved, required increased doses of Dilaudid, and began to lose the perspective of just how fortunate I was not to require surgery, not to have lost any brain function, and just how fortunate I was just to be alive.

Over the next two days, I managed to shift my attitude into a more positive place. By the end of the week, my neurosurgeon agreed that I could return home to convalesce fully a week or two sooner than his previous most optimistic estimate. I had to agree to return to the hospital for a final angiogram, which I readily agreed to. I was so happy to return home.

I hadn't had an aneurysm, and gratefully there is no lasting damage. The diagnosis is a subarachnoid hemorrhage, which, once the blood is reabsorbed, goes away. No surgery required; no brain damage incurred— incredibly good fortune against substantial odds.

I passed my final angiogram, and that afternoon, while I was recovering, the nurse who was attending to me shared that she had been running tests on me when I had first arrived at the hospital several weeks back.

She recalled a conversation she had with a technician marveling that I was still alive and that I had survived the two-and-a-half-hour ambulance medevac.

I've since been cleared to return to life as usual, though it will be early fall before I'm able to return to the vigorous exercise routine that has been a core element of my life for nearly the past 30 years.

Undergoing a near-death experience has brought about transformational change.

I have a new realization and appreciation for people's enormous capacity to help others, often in truly life-saving ways. I've seen and experienced firsthand the sacrifice, determination, and incredible loving-kindness that we as a species can be capable of.

And I've been told that my decision and choice to see the best in others resulted in transformational change in those around me. I've learned that seemingly jaded nurses who had been working the floor for 20 years began to smile, look forward to coming to work, and would check in on me even when they didn't have to because being there with me made them happy, made them feel good and appreciated, and reminded them of why they chose a helping profession to begin with.

I discovered when my mother peeled an orange that I didn't seem to want but would eat because of the kindness of her gesture that my taste buds have been revitalized. The orange was the sweetest, most fragrant flavored thing I'd ever eaten, and it seemed I was experiencing it as I would have as a three-year-old.

That same day I smelled cinnamon buns, and when I asked both my mother and my nurse about them, they both looked at me as though I was nuts. Sure enough, the cinnamon buns appeared not only on the menu but also on breakfast trays later that morning. I suffered from allergies for years and had lost a good deal of my sense of smell. That seems to have returned, and the lilacs in Maine have never smelled so good.

I offer these observations having once again experienced firsthand the power of the human spirit, our collective desire for goodness and happiness, and the incredible transformational force that comes merely by trying to see the best in others and expressing appreciation for their efforts.

The unbounded loving-kindness of friends and family that I've experienced saved my life, enriched my understanding of purpose and has reinforced my fundamental belief in the truth that the universe wants each of us to be enormously successful and that each of us has all the resources within us to successfully undertake any challenge that life presents us with—if only we decide to access the positive energy within us.

I'm looking forward to working with new and old friends for the next 30 or 40 years, and I can assure you that so much success and happiness lie ahead. I'm back to work and thrilled to have the incredibly good fortune to apply these lessons each and every day as I go about my business—personally and professionally.

Shared for what it's worth and offered with my very warmest regards.

AUTHOR BIOGRAPHY

 For the past 20 years, Jan Semba has served as advisor, facilitator, and coach working with successful people and successful organizations to help them get more of what they want and less of what they don't want.

He collaborates with clients to define and re-define strategy, and advises in governance, succession planning, developing high performance teams, and leadership development.

His experience includes executive and senior management positions in the Fortune 500 and in small and family owned companies.

Over the years, Jan has played and coached soccer competitively in both the United States and abroad. He holds an Advanced National Diploma from United Soccer Coaches (NSCAA) and has worked with men's and women's teams at the youth, Olympic Development, collegiate, and adult club level, He has run marathons, competed in triathlons, and spends much of the Maine winter alpine skiing.

Jan is a bi-racial, bilingual, first generation US citizen – son of a refugee mother and immigrant father He has three adult children.

A graduate of Hamilton College and Columbia University, Jan's work embodies his passion for developing potential.

USING THE APPENDIX

Universal Truths was written for the reader to use as inspiration and a guide as every day circumstances arise.

Patterns and themes occur and recur regularly – in life, in family, and in business.

The Appendix contains 16 patterns and themes.

Chapters associated with the patterns and themes are listed so the reader can easily choose to find an essay which may speak to the circumstance and moment at hand.

APPENDIX
PATTERNS AND THEMES

Change	1-8; 10-13; 16-19
Choice	1,2,4-8; 10-13; 19
Communication	2, 4, 10, 14, 16, 20
Control	1-6; 8; 12; 13; 19; 21
Creativity	1,2,6,13,19
Family	1,3-5; 8-18
Family Business	1-21
Genius	13, 15, 16
Habits	6-8; 10, 12,14,16, 18-20
Plan	1-5; 11, 12, 16
Pleasure/Pain	1, 3-5; 7, 9-11; 13, 14, 16-19, 21
Purpose	1-3; 5, 11, 12,15, 17
Reflect	1-4; 7, 8 ,10, 14, 18-21
Strategy	2-4; 10, 17, 19 21
Time	1,2, 11, 17
Vision	1-4

Made in the USA
Coppell, TX
28 January 2022

72511390R00049